J. S. Fletcher

Ballads of Revolt

J. S. Fletcher

Ballads of Revolt

ISBN/EAN: 9783743306066

Manufactured in Europe, USA, Canada, Australia, Japa

Cover: Foto ©Thomas Meinert / pixelio.de

Manufactured and distributed by brebook publishing software
(www.brebook.com)

J. S. Fletcher

Ballads of Revolt

Ballads of Revolt

BOOKS BY J. S. FLETCHER

LIFE IN ARCADIA (Vol. II. of the Arcady Library). Cr. 8vo. 5s. net.

THE WONDERFUL WAPENTAKE. Cr. 8vo. 5s. 6d. net.

GOD'S ¦FAILURES (Keynotes Series). Cr. 8vo. 3s. 6d. net.

LONDON : JOHN LANE, THE BODLEY HEAD.

Ballads of Revolt

BY

J. S. FLETCHER

JOHN LANE, THE BODLEY HEAD,
LONDON AND NEW YORK
1897

CONTENTS

That statue in the public square ?
Yon golden image set so high ?
And do you say that God is there ?
Why, there, methinks, you speak a lie !

And you would stay me from assault
Who come from where the linnet sings
His fiery ballads of revolt
Against conventional lies and things ?

Pull me yon statue from its place !
Break up that image into dust !
Break down those barriers 'gainst his grace
Whose gifts are hope and love and trust.

That's God !   Ho ! ye that mourn and weep,
Ho ! toilers towards the hill's steep brow,
God is not dead : God does not sleep :
Look closer !   Do you see him now ?

SO God laid him down to sleep, and I waited for his awaking.
O my belovèd. I waited, longing to bring thee glad tidings.
Full of sorrow I waited, knowing that earth in her travail
Looked and cried for my coming, who sat there with folded pinions
Waiting the waking of God, and meanwhile impotent, helpless.

And while he slept I watched, filling my mind with remembrance
Of days that are dead, glad days, when hope and joy of the morrow
And faith in the things to be swept through thy heart with the passion
And hot assurance of youth, and made thee, O my belovèd,
Brightest of all the worlds that God in his pleasure created.

I remembered the first great day, when thou wert called into being.
God's latest plaything thou wert, fashioned of refuse and wreckage,

2

Remnants of other toys that he made and
    broke ere the evening,
Out of their fragments he made thee and
    called thee perfection.
Success after failure thou wert, the thought
    and the vision made perfect.

I remembered the days of old, ere God be-
    gan to forget thee.
Thou wert my wonder, my joy : I looked
    and beheld God's fingers
Fashion thy beauty until it lay all perfect
    beneath them—
Wonder of mountain tops and of sleeping
    woods in the valley,
And music of languorous seas and silence of
    motionless oceans.

I remembered the days of old, when God
    began to forget thee.
Thou wert my charge, my delight ; for thee
    I fought with Abaddon.
For thee I wept—lo ! the steps of God
    throne bear me witness.
Fiercely with Satan I fought and prevaile
    not, for God was regardless.
He was asleep or at play, and thou and I
    were forgotten.

3

O that I might have preserved thee, belovèd,
from danger !
O that my voice might have warned thee of
evil and sorrow :
Warned thee of days to come, of the weep-
ing, the pain, and the anguish,
Wailing of woman and child, and cursing of
man, sore-stricken,
The burden of earth forgot, the burden of
earth defenceless.

But, as a child that is satiate, God turned
him at last from his plaything.
Out of his fingers he cast the strings and
the threads of direction.
Henceforth he left thee to stray and to drift,
as a feather that rises,
Blown by the wind, to the height of some
eddying current
Is swept, driven hither and thither in end-
less and purposeless circles.

Then didst thou stray from God, for he slept
and forgot thee.
In the meadows of springtide he slept, but
thou towards the forest

4

Hastening with eager feet wert quick unto
    evil and mischief,
The spirit of evil was with thee and led thee
    forth laughing
To far-off recesses of sin while God lay
    asleep in the meadow.

Then God awoke from his sleep and remem-
    bered, but thou hadst escaped him.
Far, far away in the desert, a prey to the
    wolf and the vulture,
Sad at heart didst thou sit, given over to
    hopeless despairing.
Once didst thou lift up thy voice to call upon
    God and salvation,
Once in the gathering night God caught the
    sound of thy weeping.

Then he arose and made ready and bade
    me go forth to thy succour,
Bearing the tidings of joy and news of a
    mighty redemption ;
Once more thy path should lie through the
    meadows of love and perfection,
Once more thy hand in God's and his pro-
    vidence shielding thee always,
Once more the days of old when he made
    thee and joyed in the making.

5

So to thee, earth, I came—and there to the
ears of the Virgin,
Mary, the sinless and pure, proclaimed the
great news of salvation,
Showed her the lily of God, of peace the
sweet promise and emblem,
Saw the great dawn in her eyes and the
flush of new life in her bosom,
Sunrise of hope and joy that should change
thy weeping to laughter.

Then sat I down to watch—Alas for the hope
and the promise !
Too long hadst thou strayed, too long had
God slept in the meadow.
Hearts that have strayed from each other
can never again be united.
Filled were thy eyes with dust and knew not
hope when they saw him.
Alas for the love and the promise that
blossomed and died in its fulness !

O foolish and blind that thou wert !—for
now God turned in his anger.
Wearied of thee and thy folly and of all that
his pleasure had made thee

6

Out of his heart he cast thee, concerned no
    more for thy sorrow,
Unto the hosts of hell he yielded his right
    and dominion,
Left thee to pain and despair, and lay down
    to sleep in the meadow.

But I that loved thee watched, waiting for
    his awaking.
Slow were the long, long years, and bitter
    the sound of thy weeping,
Bitter the agonised prayers, the wailing of
    spirits that perished,
Bitter the curses of men who found life's
    burden too heavy,
Bitter the crying for help to God who slept,
    hearing nothing.

O earth that God made for his pleasure and
    fashioned so strangely,
How have I wept for thee while he that
    made thee slumbered !
How have I longed to bring thee abiding
    peace and redemption,
Joy and the fulness of life, with rest from
    thy passionate striving,
How have I waited his waking, intent on
    thy final salvation !

7

And at last God woke and turned him away
from the meadow,
Through the high courts of heaven he passed
with his angels attendant,
Then fell I down at his feet beseeching his
pity and mercy,
Silent he heard me, and sat, still wrapped in
a terrible silence,
And through the silence he heard the last
faint sound of thy crying.

Then he arose and spoke and bade me go
forth with his message :
Naught was required of thee, for thou wert
too weary and feeble,
Thou hadst been tried and had failed, but
now God's mercy should save thee,
All things with thee should be new and the
past forgotten for ever ;
He would remake and remould thee and
once more call thee perfection.

So went I forth once more with news of a
blessed evangel.
Me the great stars saluted with hymns of
love and rejoicing.

8

Speed on thy errand, they cried, too long
has the earth's tribulation,
Too long has its pitiful cry for mercy re-
echoed about us,
Speed on thy errand, they cried, and sang,
rejoicing together.

So came I to thee, O earth, to cry the final
evangel !
O my belovèd, where art thou—what is it
that hides thee ?
Cold are thy fires, and black the hills and
the desolate meadows,
Silent is every village, the dead lie thick in
the city,
Nothing but Death remains and Satan
brooding beside him !

This is the end, O God, that madest earth
for thy pleasure !
This is the end of the hoped and the
promised perfection.
Sunless and moonless thou rollest, O earth,
through the heavens,
Dead is the glory of man and dead the
hopes that he clung to.
Death and Satan triumphed while God lay
asleep in the meadows.

9

THE ANGEL OF THE ANNUNCIA-TION

O my belovèd, O earth, why liest thou there so silent?
Woe is me for thy promise and woe for the peace that I brought thee.
Long, long had I waited and watched—O woe for the watching and waiting,
Cold and grey thou art, and grey and cold are thy ashes,
O earth that God made for his pleasure and left to destruction!

O my belovèd, O earth, woe is me for thy sorrow and anguish,
The wailing of waiting souls and of spirits that languished in prison.
O my belovèd, O earth, woe is me for the final evangel.
Cold and dead didst thou lie ere God rose from sleep in the meadow.
O my belovèd, O earth, woe is me for thy promise and failure!

"WELCOME, welcome, my angels all ! The
        I hold my court to-day.   Interim Report
Welcome, ye bright emissaries   •   •
That come from far away.   •
How is 't with you?   Come, tell me true
What things are said and done
In my realms afar, in each planet and star,
Come tell me true, each one."

" O I am the angel of the wind :
All's well with mine and me.
From world to world our way we take,
A jovial company !
And whither we go no man may know,
We send no warning sign,
But we come and are gone, and we sweep
        right on !
All's well with me and mine."

" O I am the angel of the rain :
All's well with mine and me.
Unto the thirsty land we pay
The tribute of the sea.
We follow the sun as his course is run,
Our shower succeeds his shine.
Lo ! the glint of our tears on the sunlit
        spheres—
All's well with me and mine."

"O I am the angel of the snow:
All's well with mine and me.
We have prisoned the earth in a warm
    white cell
Till springtide sets it free.
O sweet and rare are the things hid there,
The jewels of earth so fine,
That in every field our care's concealed—
All's well with me and mine."

"Now welcome, welcome, my angels all;
Welcome, my angels three !
'Tis well with the wind and the rain and the
    snow,
And with their ministry.
There's never a fear in star or sphere ;
Complete is the scheme divine,
And I bless the day that I can say
All's well with me and mine.

"Now joy, now joy, my angels all,
Keep holiday with me !"
But ere they turned to the smiling board
The bars dropped suddenly,
And across the space, with sorrowful face
Another angel came :
Like one amazed he stood and gazed
Ere he bowed his head in shame.

12

"O who art thou that comest thus,
In such a dreary guise?
And wherefore dost thou hang thy head
And turn away thine eyes?
Come, look this way—who art thou, say,
That dost disturb our mirth?"—
He raised his head: "I am," he said,
"The angel of the earth.

"Me centuries of years ago
Thou didst dismiss thy court,
And bade me seek the world and make
An interim report
Of all I saw, of fault and flaw,
Of things said, thought, and done
In that lonely world whose course is hurled
Around yon flaming sun."

"Now welcome, welcome, my angel dear!
Now tell thy tale to me.
And is it well with that lonely world
Which I sent thee forth to see?
Come, tell me true, how is't with you?"
The angel bowed his head:
"O woe is me that any should see
The things I have seen!" he said.

THE INTERIM
REPORT

"O angel of the howling wind,
Thou smug philosopher !
In the world that I have lately left
There's never a breeze can stir
That does not sweep where children weep,
That does not sob and sigh
O'er the living grave where strong men rave
And curse their lot and die !

"O angel of the falling rain,
I would that thou couldst see
The rain of their tears who never cease
To weep in sympathy !
But there's never a shower of thine has power
To sweep the flood away
Of that human rain of heart and brain
That flows on day by day.

"O angel of the sheltering snow,
Thou whited sepulchre !
What shouldst thou know of blackened
    hearths,
Of happy homes that were ?
How shouldst thou know that want and woe
Lie thick 'neath winter's cloud,
That thy whiteness sweet is a whiteness meet
For winding sheet and shroud ?"

14

"Nay come, nay come, my angel dear!
Wherefore dost so upbraid
The angels of my providence
Whom of my will I made?
Now let us hear some news of cheer : "
The angel bowed his head:
" O woe is me that I should see
The things I have seen !" he said.

" Nay come, nay come, I sent thee forth
A paradise to find
In that fair world which I upraised
Out of my inmost mind.
Come, tell me, then, what news of men?"
The angel bent his knee :   .
" Their lonely lot by thee forgot,
Men have forgotten thee ! "

" Nay come, nay come, my angel dear!
What wandering words are these ?
All other worlds that I have made
Have naught that does not please.
Nay now, nay now, I think that thou
Some better news must keep : "
He raised his head : " Dear God," he said,
" Let me go hence and weep ! "

15

THE INTERIM REPORT

" Nay come, nay come, my angel dear !
But wherefore weep ? " said he.
" To-day with all my shining hosts
I keep high revelry.
Come, be of cheer, my angel dear : "
He turned and from him fled :
" O woe is me that any should see
The things I have seen ! " he said.

GOD to his angels said : " How long
It is since first I made the world,
The echo of whose suppliant song
Across abysmal space is hurled !

" Sometimes as on my throne I sit,
Satiate with heaven's eternal praise,
I catch a dying strain of it,
And mind me of the long dead days.

" And yesternight, what time the stars
Were racing through the firmament,
I lifted up the golden bars
And towards that lonely world I leant.

" (Poor world, that I so long ago
With but a nod did cause to be,
And left to keep a watch of woe
Through ages of eternity !)

" I saw it there—a speck of light
That battled stoutly on its way ;
Weary, with longing for the night ;
Heart-sick, with hoping for the day.

17

"And as I leant me through the bars
Methought I heard its suppliant song
Mix with the music of the stars :
"'How long, oh God; dear God, how
long?'"

Then rose he from his golden throne :
"Herein no longer will I sit.
Is not the world I made, my own?
I will go forth and visit it."

Wherefore God came to earth ; he came
Apparelled as an emperor ;
The kings did honour to his name,
Him the great nobles bowed before.

Banquets and feasts they gave to him ;
Of cities great they made him free ;
The midnight skies were nightly dim
With perfume of their revelry.

His days in one unceasing round
Of pleasure and delight were spent,
His ears caught no offending sound,
His eyes on nothing base were bent.

In courts and gorgeous palaces
A year he passed : his soul was full
Of high content and perfect ease,
The essence of the beautiful !

Yet once or twice, when day was gone,
And the short night gave time for thought,
He minded him of things whereon
A deeper knowledge he had sought.

" Here," said he, " all is ease and joy,
The land with milk and honey teems,
The gold of life has no alloy,
The bright days droop to brighter dreams.

" But where is voiced that bitter cry?
From whom ascends that suppliant song?
' Help us, O Father, lest we die !
How long, O God, dear God, how long ? '

" I hear no wailing where I stand
Set high within these palaces ;
Here life and joy go hand in hand
With calm content and dreamful ease.

19

"Now will I lay aside my state
And make my knowledge all complete!"
He turned and passed his palace gate,
And stood, a beggar, in the street.

Then saw he with a vague regret
That men had long forgot his grace;
They had torn him from their hearts, and set
A golden image in his place.

All night he wandered here and there,
And lo! with the returning day,
'Midst the grey rain, the chilling air,
The destitute and homeless lay!

He stayed amidst that ghastly throng,
His quick ear caught their whispered sigh!
"How long, oh God? Dear God, how long?
Sweet Father, help us, lest we die!"

Then rose his soul in fiery zeal:
"Is this the earth that once I made?
Now for the sick world's common weal
I go to preach the great crusade!"

He stood within the market place :
" Ho, ye that love the good, the true !
Stay with me for a little space,
I have a thing to say to you."

The world went by with sneer and jest ;
He turned and passed through street and
    square.
" Will no one listen ? "   His behest
Fell empty on the careless air.

Then turned he to the palaces :
" Here am I sure of sympathy !
Living themselves in such sweet ease,
They needs must feel for them that die."

He stood before an emperor—
" Lay down thy crown and come with me ! "
They haled him to the palace door,
And thrust him forth with mockery.

Then woke revolt within his heart ;
He stirred the people to debate ;
He made them feel wrong's stinging smart ;
He taught them how to scorn and hate.

THE
VISITATION

From land to land he went. "Arise!
Awake!" he cried. "To-day shall see
The lightening of the longing eyes,
The freeing of the would-be free!"

Then rose the mighty and the strong:
"Or fool or knave thou art!" they said.
They slew him 'midst a gaping throng,
And on a high place set his head.

So mingled he with earth at last:
No human hand his dust may find:
His body in the fire they cast,
And flung his ashes to the wind.

NOW when they told her that the end The
   Was drawing near and soon must be: Last Sacrament
"Content," she said: "but, pray you, send
My chaplain from the Monast'ry.

"Bid him to leave his quiet cell
For one brief hour and hither haste.
So there's no hope, good leech? Ah, well,
Of hell or heaven I soon shall taste!"

By dripping lane and wind-swept moor
The groaning palfrey ambled till
The chaplain panted at her door:
"And is my lady living still?"

"Now clear the chamber! Chaplain, come;
Sit here, where I can see thee; I,
That on these matters long was dumb,
Must speak about them ere I die."

They cleared the room. "Say naught," he
      said,
"But that of sin thou dost repent,
That thou may'st die, much comforted,
By comfortable sacrament."

23

" Nay, chaplain, chaplain, sit thee here,
Nor stay me from what I would say:
Thou canst not raise in me one fear
Of what may chance ere break of day ! "

He crossed himself ; he sat him down ;
She laid her lily hand in his :
" There's many a king would give his crown
That little hand," she said, " to kiss."

" Bethink thee, lady !   O confess
Thy sin and bend a lowly head
Before God's awful bar ! "   " Ah, yes ;
But my sin was so sweet," she said.

" Come tell me, chaplain, tell me true,
Thou who art old and gnarled and thin,
When thou wast young, didst never do
Some sin that did not seem a sin ?

" And chaplain, bend thee down—I know
That thou hast crushed the things that were
From out thy heart, and now art slow
To let the mad blood in thee stir.

24

" But I—nay, chaplain, dry thy tears !
What matter, after all, that I,
A thing of twenty careless years,
Should leave my happiness and die ?

" But chaplain, hast thou never thought
How good it is to feel so gay ?
To feel that all that's good is brought
Into the compass of one day ?

" And chaplain, didst thou never feel,
As thou didst roam in field or wood,
Sweet madness through thy fancies steal,
Sweet promptings fire thy waking blood ?

"And chaplain, chaplain, tell me true,
As thou wert on thine own death-bed,
Now tell me quick, what must I do ?
For oh, it was so sweet !" she said.

" Oh lady, lady, turn thy thought
Away from sin and list to me,
For sin with heavy pain is fraught— "
" But then it was so sweet !" said she.

25

THE LAST
SACRAMENT

"And then, I was so young and glad!"
"Thou dying soul," he cried, "Repent!"
"Oh chaplain, but the world was mad
That day with springtide's merriment."

"Besides, I loved him so! ah, well;
But chaplain, chaplain, tell me true,
And must one lie in deepest hell
For doing what one so wished to do?

"And, tell me, chaplain, tell me this:
Why we unsatisfied should pass
The trysting place, when springtide's kiss
Made happy dimples in the grass?

"Oh chaplain, when to-night is o'er
Will those sweet memories be fled?
Will recollection be no more?
For, oh, it was so sweet!" she said.

"Now rest thee, rest thee, troubled soul,
Pour out thy secret sin to me.
Christ's mercy yet shall make thee whole—"
"But then it was so sweet!" said she.

26

Her eyelids drooped, she seemed to sleep, SACRAMENT
Her failing breath came soft and slow ;
" O chaplain, chaplain, do not weep !
It was so sweet," she murmured low.

" O come again, sweet twilight hour ! "
Her eyelids closed : upon her breast,
Folded about a faded flower,
Her lily hands she laid to rest.

" Now draw the sheet about my face,
And sit thee, chaplain, by the bed.
Ah, chaplain, not for all God's grace
Would I exchange this flower ! " she said.

Uprose the wind about her walls,
The storm came roaring at her gate :
" Lady, awake !—the angel calls ;
Repent thee, ere it be too late ! "

Across the moor the thunder rolled,
The chaplain's palfrey screamed with fear.
" Alack ! she is so stark and cold !
O lady, lady, dost thou hear ?

THE LAST SACRAMENT

"Repent thee! Christ, who died for men
Waits, all-forgiving, at thy side;
Repent thee of thy sin!"—"But then
It was so sweet," she said and died.

NOW when from utter nothingness
The world's wild heart woke up to beat
Its rhythm of pleasure and distress,
In harmonies of sad and sweet,

An angel at God's side said " Lo,
I leave thy brightness for the shade
Wherein lie other worlds : I go
To see the wonders thou hast made."

Forthwith toward the unknown things
Of limitless space he flew.   The bars
Of heaven were dropped.   His rapid wings
Caught the first glory of the stars.

Through belts of dazzling lights he passed,
Through darkened gulfs himself he hurled,
He spurned the sun and moon—at last
He lighted on the new-made world.

'Twas in that season when the sedge
Shields the shy iris from the sun,
When trees are green, and every hedge
Proclaims the springtide feasts begun.

Joy was abroad with love and mirth,
They made a jocund company.
He watched them pass, and felt the earth
To be a thing right good to see.

In all God's work he found no flaw,
Nothing to him seemed void or vain,
And on a summer's eve he saw
Two lovers kissing in a lane.

Thereat rose in him enviousness:
" In all God's heaven no mate have I !
Nothing against my heart may press
Its mute appeal for sympathy."

He looked once more: he saw the light
Of virginal love in human eyes
In all its sweetness.   At the sight
He rose and fled across the skies.

" Make me a man !" he prayed.   In heaven
God caused within him a new birth,
Straightway he clove the star-strewn leven,
And stood a man upon the earth.

He found a mate—against his breast
He prisoned love and bound it fast.
" Here," said he, " will I take my rest ;
My life is perfected at last."

New charms he found in night and day;
New passions filled his heart with flame,
No memory within him lay
Of that far heaven from whence he came.

From the red sunrise till the night
He toiled and strove in dust and sweat,
But never to the worlds of light
Turned once with longing or regret.

So through the ever-rolling years
He lived and loved and toiled, and still
Of the wild joy. the grief and tears,
Of human life he took his fill.

Then from high heaven God spoke to him :
" Thou art my angel, and thy place
'Midst cherubim and seraphim
Is empty.   Of my pitying grace

"I gave thee human life and lo!
Love hast thou had, and joy, and peace,
And all good things of earth, but know
That these are transient; they will cease.

"Man is but mortal. Would'st thou die?
Thee my full love encompasseth.
Choose now 'twixt heaven's eternity
And life—and life's sure ending, death."

Thereat he fell on sleep. God made
A vision pass before his eyes,
Once more he crossed the worlds of shade
And took his place in Paradise.

The long, long days of calm delight
Flowed round him like a tideless sea,
Nothing had power his soul to fright
With creeping fears of what might be.

Then turned he to the earth: he saw
Life turned to living death; the tears
That follow in unchanging law
The dying laughter of the years.

Partings of them that would not part; THE LOST ANGEL
Sobbings of lovers loth to go;
Heart sundered from its sister heart;
The great world's untranslated woe;

All these he heard and saw.   "Afar
There waits me sweet eternity,
Filled with unchanging peace, but ah!
In all God's heaven no mate have I."

He woke: it was a summer eve;
His children from the woodland ran;
He stretched his arms: "Why should I
    grieve?
I am very man of very man!"

He turned him to his cottage door:
" Sweetheart, how long the day has been!
Say, dost thou love me more and more?
My heart's true solace and my queen?"

He drew her, longing, to his breast:
" Thy love," he said, "is more than all!"
There, while God's glory filled the west,
They kept love's tireless festival.

33

Then sank the sun; uprose the moon;
The stars came peeping in the sky.
His dear ones slept. "Thanks for thy boon!
Life have I known in verity!"

"Henceforth I am of mortal birth."
He turned him to the star-strewn leven—
"Better this day of love on earth
Than centuries of life in heaven!"

So it was driven upon his mind
   That he should go apart from them
Who strove with world-worn chains to bind
The intent of God in Bethlehem.

The wondering mother looked and saw,
And nothing said of her distress—
Behind his keeping of the law
Rose youthful manhood's restlessness.

He kept the feast, he kept the fast,
There was no flaw in him to see ;
None might reprove him, but at last
Within his soul rose heresy.

As by the workshop bench he stood,
Or wandered 'neath the village wall,
The fires of youth shot through his blood
And through his spirit virginal.

Delicious promptings to him came,
Strange questionings, and vague delight ;
His heart grew hot with shy, sweet shame ;
There was new glamour in the night.

35

THE
SCAPEGOAT

He looked, he saw, and suddenly
The heart of life in him began
To beat with newer ecstacy,
And with the force of very man.

So, filled with human hope and fear,
He progressed through the dreamy days,
Till in the springtide of the year
He reached the parting of the ways.

Behind him lay the sun-kissed track,
The skies how clear! the grass how green!
"No more," he said, "may I go back;
Nothing can be as it has been."

Before him stretched the wilderness,
Wrapped in a dreary gloom it lay;
"Here lies my path"—in loneliness
He turned him to the unknown way.

And in the midst of that wild waste
His spirit waxed full hot with strife:
"Oh, Thou who Art!" he cried, "make haste,
Haste, haste, and tell me what is Life!

"Tell me the secret of my heart,
Show me, as in a scroll unfurled,
The hidden Truth ! O, Thou who Art,
Read me the riddle of the world."

The grey mists vanished suddenly ;
From the high peaks there came a voice :
"Behold the world ! Look out, and see,
And of thy choices make thy choice."

He looked, he saw, no breath he drew :
The vision burnt his soul like flame.
"Or art thou false, or art thou true,
O awfulness that hast no Name?"

Life in its myriad forms he saw,
The shifting of its light and shade,
Its half-perfection, and its flaw,
He saw, unmoved and undismayed.

He saw the pride and pomp of earth ;
The golden promise of an hour ;
Sorrow and joy ; despair and mirth ;
The sweets of undisputed power.

37

THE
SCAPEGOAT

He watched men rise ; he saw them fall ;
He saw life wander like a breath
From this to that.   Behind it all
Lay the weird shade whose name is Death.

The vision passed : upon his ear
From that high summit fell the voice :
" Once more behold ! Before thee here
Lie the two paths—make thou thy choice."

He looked, he saw—before him lay,
As in a mighty scroll unfurled,
The power and pomp of life's short day,
The purple kingdoms of the world.

All manner of delight lay spread
Before him with alluring guile :
The harlot in her perfumed bed,
The sweetness of a bride's shy smile.

O dear delight of life ! O sweet,
Sweet happiness of dreamy days,
And dreamier nights, where all things meet
To crowd with joy the primrose ways !

O pride of power, O maddening lust
Of fierce desire to rule and bind,
To hold the mighty world in trust,
One's self the sole, the master-mind !

" All these are thine—love, wisdom, power:
Thine with an uncontrolled control,
What, wouldst thou hesitate one hour ?
The price ?   Why, nothing—but thy soul.

" Thy soul !—a miserable thing
That profits naught, that keeps thee poor,
That bids thee sigh when others sing,
And turns thee from thy mistress' door.

"Thy soul?—why, perhaps thou hast no soul?
'Twas but a lie thy fathers taught.
Let the world go, the quick years roll,
Eat, drink, be merry, care for naught.

" Take pleasure as it comes, and range
The honied sweetnesses of sin ;
One hour of such were rich exchange
For thy poor soul, so starved and thin.

39

" Besides, thou hast no soul ! O fool,
Wilt thou prefer to power and ease
The hardness of some iron rule,
Because of idle dreams like these?

" Let the world go—what need for thee
To starve thy life and be denied?
Now is the time for liberty!
Live !—make thy longings satisfied."

He turned, he saw the evening star
Rise slowly o'er the night's wide hem,
And in the moonlight's glow, afar,
The white-walled house in Bethlehem.

" The other way ! "   Across the skies
He cried once more,   " Now let me see
That other way ! "   With patient eyes
He stood in calm expectancy.

Ah, who shall say what there he sees,
Or what wild phantoms twist and toss
Their dismal shapes about his knees
To drag him from the destined Cross?

40

" O life that seemed so fair and sweet !
O life that I henceforth must live !
O mysteries that in me meet !
O mystery that will forgive ! "

All night he wept—at last the sun
Filled with new light the morning skies.
" Amen ! " he said. " It is begun :
Let the new man in me arise !

" Die, all that I could wish to be ! ,
Live, all that I henceforth must prove !
Farewell, wild thoughts of liberty !
Welcome, fierce travail of my love ! "

The flaming sun was high o'erhead ;
The skies were like a scroll unfurled.
He stood erect : " I go," he said,
" To be the scapegoat of the world."

His mother met him at the door
Of that white house in Bethlehem :
" Sweet mother, sweeter than before ! "
He stooped and kissed her garment's hem.

41

THE
SCAPEGOAT

And so across the land he passed,
Warming men's hearts with subtle flame,
And human sweetness, till at last
The hour of expiation came.

Then woke the world with sudden stir.
"Whence came this power our hearts to
    draw?
Call ye this man a carpenter?
He is a God!" they cried in awe.

Ah me, it was no God they hailed,
No arbiter of life and death,
But a poor man who dared and failed,
A carpenter of Nazareth.

Failed? Aye, for still the nations bend
To their false gods a servile knee,
And still the scapegoat finds his end
On the dark heights of Calvary.

But here and there upon the sun
Some man still fixes dauntless eyes,
And says "Amen!   It is begun;
Let the new life in me arise!"

Printed by R. Folkard & Son,
22, Devonshire St., Queen Sq., London.

www.ingramcontent.com/pod-product-compliance
Lightning Source LLC
Chambersburg PA
CBHW032120080426
42733CB00008B/999